Summer Flower

MARK J. WESTON

Flower arrangements by Jane Weston

Photography by Roger Tuff

THE FOUR SEASONS PUBLISHING COMPANY (IRELAND) LTD.
26 Fitzwilliam Square, Dublin 2

Main U.K. Distributors: FOUR SEASONS PUBLICATIONS
The Stables, Monxton, Nr. Andover, Hants, SP11 8AT.

© FOUR SEASONS PUBLICATIONS

SBN 901131 00 8

PREFACE

Every flower arrangement is an individual and unique work of art in it's own right and the subtle combination of various flower shapes and colours provide endless opportunities for creating beautiful and original compositions.

But, as with every other art or craft, it is necessary to acquire the knowledge of basic techniques before flowers can be arranged tastefully and to their best advantage.

This book illustrates, by the use of a unique step-by-step photographic analysis method, how to assemble seventeen different summer flower arrangements. All the flowers used in the arrangements can be readily and inexpensively obtained, during their appropriate flowering seasons, direct from your local flower shop. No longer is it necessary to sacrifice the beauty of the garden so that the flowers can be supplied for house decoration.

Flower arranging is a pastime that brings peace of mind from the hurly burly of the daily routine and is justifiably rated as the most popular leisure time activity amongst discriminating people. If you already arrange flowers you may find some new and interesting ideas and suggestions in this book. If, however, you still have not plunged into this exciting and creative activity you will find that this book will supply you with the basic information needed to employ your inherent artistic ability to the full.

MARK J. WESTON

CONTENTS

EQUIPMENT

"Oasis"

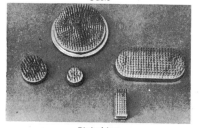

Pinholders

"Oasis" is a water absorbent plastic foam which is available from your flower shop in several shapes and sizes. Flower stems inserted into "Oasis" are held firmly in position. It should be well soaked in water before use and can be cut with a table knife to the required size. After the flowers have been arranged it is important to keep the "Oasis" continually moist by adding water. When the flowers are finally spent the "Oasis" can be used for subsequent arrangements. There are other plastic foam mounts available such as "Florapak" and "Stemfix" but "Oasis" has been used for all the arrangements in this book.

Pinholders in many shapes and sizes are available from your flower shop. They are a useful substitute for "Oasis" particularly when line arrangements in shallow dishes are required. They can also be used in conjunction with "Oasis" or wire-netting (see below).

Chicken Wire. 2" chicken wire-netting is also an inexpensive flower arranging medium. It should be cut from the roll and crumpled up before insertion into the container.

Scissors. When arranging flowers it is most desirable to use a pair of special flower scissors. These have one blade with a serrated edge designed to stop the scissors from slipping on the flower stem. They are readily available from your flower shop.

CONTAINERS

The selection of the container for any flower arrangement is governed by its general suitability both to the flowers which are to be used and the type of arrangement.

In this book, although seventeen different arrangements are portrayed, only seven different easy-to-come-by containers are used. Any of these containers can be substituted for one of a somewhat similar size and shape. All of these containers are inexpensive and should be available at your flower shop.

"Oasis" Dish & Copper Jug

Oasis Dish. These inexpensive plastic dishes are available in two sizes. The large dish, which has been used for several arrangements in this book, has four small spikes incorporated in the base. A portion of "Oasis" can be cut from the block and held in position by these projections.
This container is most suitable for Line, Triangular, All-the-way-round and L shaped arrangements.

Copper Jug. This small jug, owing to its curved shape, is particularly suitable for the Assymetrical type of arrangement. It needs to be filled with part of a block of "Oasis" (not crumbled) before use.

Boat Shaped Basket with handle

Boat shaped Basket with handle. This basket has a metal lining filled with "Oasis". It is most suitable for the Crescent or L shaped arrangements, with the curved handle playing a complementary role.

Rectangular Basket. With the metal lining filled with "Oasis" it is most suitable for a Triangular or L shaped flower arrangement. The straight lines of this basket make it unsuitable for the curved type of arrangements.

Rectangular Basket

Round Basket with Lid

Rectangular Basket with Handle &
Hamper Basket with lid

Round Basket with lid. Owing to the compensating curves, this container is particularly relevant to the Crescent arrangement, with the lid acting as a background.

Rectangular Basket with handle. This is complete with metal lining. Useful for the Triangular or All-the-way-round arrangements. The graceful handle will form an integral part of the arrangement.

Hamper Basket with lid. This is a container which is mostly confined to the L shaped arrangement, allowing the lid to act as a background to the flowers.

WIRING FLOWERS

Although it is desirable to use the natural curves of the flower stems whenever possible, sometimes this is impracticable. Under these circumstances it is necessary to make use of wires, in order to support the stem. After a flower has been wired the stem can be moulded to the required shape which will then be retained. 22 gauge 14" wires are used for this purpose and are usually available from your flower shop.

Wiring a carnation

1. A 22° ×14" wire being inserted into the base of the calyx.

2. The wire is wound around the stem of the carnation.

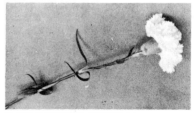

3. Wired carnation ready for use.

LINE ARRANGEMENT *(see cover)*

Ingredients
7 peonies
(Sarah Bernhardt).

1. 2 peonies have been inserted at the back of an 'Oasis' plastic dish. The height of each has been graduated.

2. 2 more peonies have been incorporated, gradually working downwards.

3. 1 slightly open peony has been recessed (close to the 'Oasis' base) and forms the focal point of the arrangement.

The Sarah Bernhardt peony, which is used in this arrangement, has like all other peonies, a very short natural flowering season. It is possible however for the flowers to be cut in precisely the right condition and to be stored in a cold room for several weeks before marketing. The flowers come to no harm as a result of this refrigeration and your florist is able to offer this charming and beautiful harbinger of summer over a much extended season.

4. The remaining 2 peonies are added to provide balance. Peony foliage, in front of container, shows relative size before incorporation.

5. 7 pieces of foliage have been incorporated, covering the 'Oasis' and the front of the container.

TRIANGULAR ARRANGEMENT

Ingredients
19 sweet williams   9 campanula
7 carnations   6 sprigs pittosporum

1. A plastic dish containing a small cube of 'Oasis' with 9 campanula forming the outline of an equilateral triangle.

2. 11 stems of sweet william complete the outline including those which project over the front of the container.

3. 8 more sweet william have now been added to commence the filling-in of the central part of the arrangement.

4. 7 carnations have now been incorporated to complete the filling-in and provide a dominant feature for the arrangement.

5. 6 sprigs of pittosporum foliage fill up any small gaps and hide any of the 'Oasis' still remaining visible.

Most flower arrangements require the use of foliage to fill up any remaining gaps when the final flowers have been incorporated. Many of the summer foliages are not really suitable for this purpose because they are not 'bushy' enough. In addition to pittosporum the following could be used instead. Box, forsythia, hosta leaves, golden and green privet and beech.

10 white carnations
10 pieces of beech

ARRANGEMENT

3. Three carnations incorporated. No. 1 establishes left hand outline. No. 2 helps to give arrangement depth. No. 3 projects 3" over the front.

2. Two more carnations have been added. The length of each stem is getting gradually shorter.

1. Using a plastic 'Oasis' container two carnations have been inserted. The taller establishes the final height of the arrangement.

Although this special but inexpensive plastic 'Oasis' container has been used for this line arrangement, it would be quite satisfactory to use any shallow dish. As an ordinary dish has no built-in facility to take an 'Oasis' block it would be necessary to use a pin holder instead which would be heavy enough (or have a suction pad) to remain in position without further support. The dish should be deep enough to allow the pin holder to be covered by water.

5. 10 pieces of beech (various lengths) have been used to mask the carnation stems and hide the 'Oasis'.

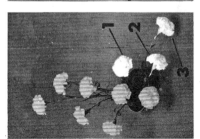

4. The remaining three carnations have been added and continue the downward and outward flow.

ALL-THE-WAY-ROUND ARRANGEMENT

Ingredients
28 stems of alstromeria
(Dover Orange)

5 stems of spray chrysanthemum
(breaking down into 15 heads
and 11 buds)

1. An 'Oasis' plastic dish is used to take the outline of 14 alstromeria stems and 7 chrysanthemum buds.

2. 14 stems of alstromeria are added to the centre part. No. 9 is $2\frac{1}{2}$ times the overall height of the container.

3. 3 chrysanthemum heads and 3 buds have been added to the outline to give it more authority.

4. 6 more chrysanthemum heads and 1 bud have been incorporated into the main body of the arrangement.

5. The remaining 6 chrysanthemum heads have been added to fill up the centre completely.

As a result of world-wide research, which is constantly being carried out by flower growers, chrysanthemum blooms and sprays are now grown and are available every day throughout the year. Owing to their very good lasting properties and extensive colour range they represent extremely good value and are a boon to the flower arranger.

Alstromeria has also been the subject of a research programme and hybridisation has enabled it to be available not only throughout most of the year but also to extend the colour range to many subtle pastel shades.

TRIANGULAR ARRANGEMENT

Ingredients
8 Nymph roses (having two or more buds)
5 Baccarat roses
9 Super Star roses
3 rose leaves

1. Using a plastic container with 'Oasis', 4 Super Star and 1 Nymph supply the outline.

2. 4 Baccarat, 2 Super Star and 3 Nymph roses have been added to fill in the outline. 8 and 9 project forwards about 3''.

3. 1 Super Star and 3 Nymph roses have been incorporated to start the filling-in process.

4. 1 Baccarat, 2 Super Star and 1 Nymph are the remaining flowers to be added to the arrangement.

5. 3 stems of rose leaves have been inserted to cover any visible 'Oasis'.

In order for roses to last well it is essential to make sure that water is taken continually up the stem. Cut about 1'' off the bottom of the stem slantwise with a sharp knife, scrape away the outer bark for $\frac{1}{2}$ inch and immerse immediately in deep, cold water. After an hour the water will have been taken up, helped by the syphon created by the depth of water. The roses are now ready to be arranged but should not be removed from the water until the last moment.

L-SHAPED ARRANGEMENT

Ingredients
7 carnations

16 double stock
10 larkspur

1. A plastic container with 'Oasis' has an outline of 7 larkspur incorporated to establish the overall height and width.

2. 4 stems of stock and 2 larkspur have been used to partially complete the left-hand outline.

3. 5 stems of stock complete the left-hand outline and commence the substantiation of the remainder of the L shape.

4. 1 larkspur, 2 stock and 1 carnation are added. Another carnation, cut very short, is inserted into the corner of the L.

5. 5 more double stock are used to fill in.

6. Finally 5 carnations are incorporated to complete the arrangement and add visual impact.

ASYMMETRICAL CURVE

Ingredients
13 dianthus   7 scabious buds
7 scabious   6 Carole roses

1. A jug filled with 'Oasis' is used for this arrangement. 6 dianthus provide the basic outline and the overall width.

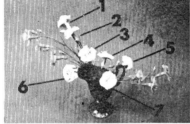

2. 7 dianthus are incorporated. The two curves have now been linked together back and front.

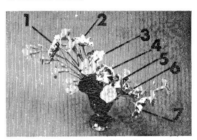

3. 7 scabious have been used in order to commence the filling-in process.

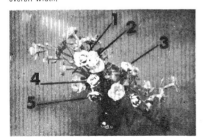

4. 6 Carole roses complete the filling-in and help to mask the 'Oasis'.

5. 7 scabious buds have been incorporated at random to lessen any tendency towards severe formality.

In this arrangement, the dianthus and scabious will not last long. They are however charming and inexpensive ingredients and represent good value. The main factor which governs the price of a flower is the expense and difficulty of its cultivation. An orchid, which takes many months of skilled care to bring it to the flowering stage will obviously cost more than a quick flowering annual—but the orchid will last much longer and therefore represents equally good value. This equation between lasting properties and price generally prevails.

TRIANGULAR ARRANGEMENT

Ingredients
11 carnations
12 Baccarat roses

1. A wicker basket with handle containing 'Oasis' is used for this arrangement. 5 Baccarat provide the commencement of the outline.

2. 4 more roses have been added to complete the outline.

3. One rose commences the filling-in procedure. The other 2 roses and 2 carnations are used to establish the front of the arrangement.

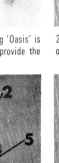

4. 5 more carnations have been incorporated and continue the filling-in process.

5. 4 more carnations have been added and complete the triangular arrangement.

Carnations are available in your flower shop virtually every day of the year in a wide range of colours. They usually last very well indeed but when the weather is thundery, they will curl up' and go over prematurely.

In order to make sure that water goes up the stems, cut $\frac{1}{2}''$ off the bottom slantwise with a sharp knife or scissors just before arranging. This removes the congealed sap at the very bottom of the stem and allows the unclogged capillaries to draw up the essential water.

CRESCENT ARRANGEMENT

Ingredients
24 Roselandia roses
11 pieces of beech

1. Using a round basket with lid, filled with a block of 'Oasis' the outline has been commenced using 7 roses.

2. 5 more roses have been used. One rose establishes the height of the arrangement and the remaining 4 complete the outline.

3. 6 roses have been incorporated and are gradually filling-in the main body of the arrangement.

4. The remaining 6 roses complete the build-up to the single rose used to establish the height of the arrangement in step '2'.

5. 11 pieces of beech foliage have been used to fill up any gaps and to completely hide the 'Oasis'.

Roses cut from the garden not only tend to rob a place of beauty but also are usually too woody in the stem to take up water satisfactorily. Commercially grown roses, lavished with skill and tended with expert care, are, on the other hand, much more inclined to drink the water and thereby last better. A wide variety of colours and sizes combined with year round availability enable the keen flower arranger to use this flower successfully on numerous occasions.

DIAGONAL ARRANGEMENT

Ingredients
12 marguerites
3 marguerite buds

8 wirral supreme
4 sprays of forsythia foliage

1. 5 marguerites and 2 marguerite buds form the top part of the arrangement in a plastic dish with an 'Oasis' block.

2. 2 more marguerites and 2 wirral have been used to form the lower part of the arrangement.

3. 1 marguerite and 1 wirral complete the diagonal. 3 wirral with 1 marguerite and 1 marguerite bud complete the outline.

4. 3 marguerites and 2 wirral have been incorporated to fill in the centre of the arrangement.

5. 4 sprigs of forsythia foliage have been used to fill in any gaps and mask the 'Oasis'.

Really fresh flowers are very thirsty and drink a lot of water particularly in hot weather, when there is also a high evaporation rate. Consequently 'Oasis' or similar plastic stem holders should be continually kept moist by adding cold water. When chicken wire or pin holders are used the water level should be kept topped up (not changed). As flowers tend to develop more quickly in high temperatures keep your arrangements out of direct sun, out of draughts and in the coolest place possible.

TRIANGULAR ARRANGEMENT

Ingredients
16 delphiniums
7 campanula
11 peonies
12 carnations
4 pieces of peony foliage

1. Using an oblong basket, filled with 'Oasis', 13 stems of delphinium and 7 campanula have been used to commence the outline.

2. 8 peonies have been added. Two of these project over the front of the container and the remainder provide substance to the outline.

3. 3 peony and 3 delphinium have been incorporated to commence the filling-in process.

4. 6 carnations further amplify the filling-in process which starts at the outside and works towards the centre.

5. 6 more carnations have been incorporated to nearly complete the arrangement.

6. 4 bits of peony foliage (from some of the peonies previously incorporated), have been used as gap fillers.

ALL-THE-WAY-ROUND ARRANGEMENT

Ingredients
50 sweet peas
20 dianthus

(note sweet peas used in this arrangement are rather small. If bigger ones are available fewer will be required).

1. Using a round plastic 'Oasis' dish, 12 sweet peas provide an outline and one central flower establishes the height.

2. 8 sweet peas and 11 dianthus have been used to fill in the outline.

3. 9 dianthus have been used to commence filling-in between the central point and the outline.

4. 12 sweet peas have been incorporated to continue the filling-in operation.

5. 9 more sweet peas have been used for further filling-in.

6. 9 sweet peas complete the arrangement. Some sweet peas have been used instead of the usual foliage for filling up gaps.

L-SHAPED ARRANGEMENT

Ingredients
9 chrysanthemum heads
(from 2–3 stems of Shasta A.Y.R.)   14 Garnet roses

1. Using a wicker hamper with lid, 3 garnet roses and 2 shasta chrysanthemums together provide the three extremities of the arrangement.

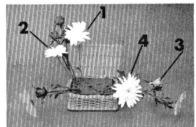

2. 1 rose and 3 chrysanthemums have been used to further substantiate the extremities.

3. 5 roses have been incorporated to gradually fill-in the outline.

4. 5 more roses have been used as fillers-in and the 'L' shape is becoming better established.

5. 4 chrysanthemums complete the filling-in and finalise the arrangement. No foliage is required because the rose leaves have provided sufficient.

Much research has gone into the subject of making flowers last longer by using chemical flower preservatives without avail. Glucose, however, when added to the water at the rate of one teaspoonful per pint can sometimes provide advantageous results. The old fashioned idea of using an aspirin or copper coin can be effective to the extent of cutting down the bacterial action which tends to clog the bottom of the flower stems. 'Oasis' and other plastic mounts usually have sufficient formaldehyde incorporated to provide a modicum of bacteria-cide without further addition.

TRIANGULAR ARRANGEMENT

Ingredients
18 carnations

10 pieces of gypsophila,
(Bristol Fairy)

1. 9 carnations provide a triangular outline in the large size of 'Oasis' dish.

2. 5 more carnations have been added. No. 3 is slightly recessed and forms a focal point.

3. The remaining 4 carnations fill in the centre of the arrangement. No. 4 has been cut short and masks the 'Oasis'.

4. 10 pieces of gypsophila are added to provide lightness, as the carnations, on their own, appear rather heavy and stiff.

Research indicates that discriminating people are becoming increasingly averse to the use of artificial flowers. When beautiful fresh flowers and plants are readily available at modest cost throughout the year, it does seem to be unnecessary to indulge in ridiculous hocus pocus. Restaurants, hotels and offices undoubtedly lower the tone of their establishments by the use of plastic flowers and no doubt jeopardise their reputation for integrity. Eating places, which have been decorated in this unfortunate fashion, bring doubting thoughts. Is the butter really margarine? What about the chicken (or is it rabbit) curry? Idleness, meanness or lack of taste can each provide an inadequate reason for the substitution of real flowers. Flower lovers should take every opportunity of rebelling against these insulting deceptions.

ASYMMETRICAL CURVE

Ingredients
18 Garnet roses
 3 rose leaf clusters

1. 6 Garnet roses are arranged in an 'Oasis' filled jug to establish the top and bottom curves of the arrangement.

2. 4 more roses continue to create an outline in accordance with the contours of the jug.

3. 3 more Garnet roses finalise the outline.

4 The 5 remaining roses have been incorporated and fill in the rest of the arrangement.

5. 3 rose leaf clusters are finally added to mask the 'Oasis' and fill up any small gaps.

Sometimes roses and other woody stemmed flowers droop their heads because water is not going up the stem even though this has been cut and split.

Under these circumstances, the roses should be re-cut and the stems placed for a few minutes in two inches of boiling water. This will relieve the air lock and the flowers will be given a new lease of life and can be rearranged.

LINE ARRANGEMENT

Ingredients
8 gladioli
4 gladioli leaves
4 sprigs of forsythia foliage

1. 2 gladioli have been inserted at the back of a plastic 'Oasis' dish—one stepped slightly below the other.

2. This picture shows the unopened florets detached from the main gladioli stem ready to incorporate into the arrangement as 'tops'.

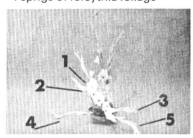

3. 2 gladioli and 3 'tops' supply the outline. The 'tops' reduce the size of the gladioli and supplement the original ingredients.

4. 4 gladioli and 1 'top' are incorporated. The open florets help fill in the centre part of the arrangement

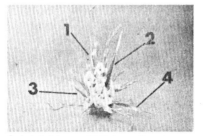

5. 4 gladioli leaves with their spearlike appearance provide a contrast in the outline.

6. 4 sprigs of forsythia foliage fill up any remaining gaps and complete the arrangement

CRESCENT ARRANGEMENT

Ingredients
9 miniature gladioli
12 Roselandia roses
7 carnations
½ bunch of outdoor chrysanthemum spray

1 9 gladioli form the commencement of the outline, following the contours of the basket and using their natural curves.

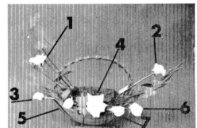

2. 7 roses complete the crescent outline. No. 4 is an open rose which will provide a centre of interest.

3. 5 more roses have been inserted at the rear to complete the three dimensional outline.

4. 7 carnations have been used to start the filling-in process. It is important to graduate the heights of the carnations.

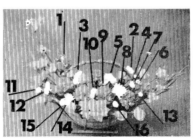

5. The stems of chrysanthemum are broken down and single heads and buds are used to complete the arrangement.

There are no precise rules concerning the use of colour. On the whole complementary colours (those which are near to one another in the rainbow spectrum) go well together. Sometimes the use of a startling contrasting colour can provide dramatic effect, particularly in modern contemporary surroundings. The best teacher is the art gallery where the ideas of well known master painters can be noted for future use.

OTHER TITLES AVAILABLE

SERIES I
Spring Flower Arranging
Autumn Flower Arranging
Winter Flower Arranging

These books show in detail the elaborate assembly techniques required to produce arrangements with a professional polish. Also many valuable hints and tips on flowers and flower decoration are given.

SERIES II
Party Flower Arranging
Church Flower Arranging
Dried Flower Arranging
Christmas Flower Arranging

These books are the companion volumes with Christmas Flower Arranging and are full of interesting information as well as a large number of sophisticated flower decorations.

FLORISTRY SERIES

The Art of Floristry—Wedding Flowers
The Art of Floristry—Funeral Flowers

These two books are each illustrated with over 400 step-by-step photographs showing the intricate techniques required to make up all types of wedding bouquets, headdresses etc, as well as funeral tributes.

Wedding Flowers in Colour
Gift and Sympathy Flowers in Colour

Two design books showing a comprehensive range of Wedding Flowers, Funeral Tributes and Gift Flowers—all in full colour.